THE OFFIC

MW00615145

LIVE LONG, DIE SHORT

A GUIDE TO AUTHENTIC HEALTH AND SUCCESSFUL AGING

by Roger Landry, MD, MPH

MAIN
IDEA
PRESS

This is a uniquely written summary accompanied by a commentary of an original book and as such references are made to the original. The author cites and acknowledges the full copyright of the original author, book, and publisher for purposes that do not pertain to fair use guidelines under the US and international copyright laws. The information in this book is in general reference to the original and for educational purposes only.

Published by Main Idea Press
Austin, TX
www.greenleafbookgroup.com

Distributed by Main Idea Press

Design and composition by Greenleaf Book Group
Cover design by Greenleaf Book Group

Print ISBN: 978-0-9980112-0-2

eBook ISBN: 978-0-9980112-1-9

First Edition

CONTENTS

SYNOPSIS

Live Long, Die Short has an important message: How we age is up to us. The choices that we make every day determine if the third stage of our lives will be a period of long, expensive, and degrading decline or a time of continued growth and highest possible functioning for as long as possible. We can take small steps each day to ensure that we are functioning at our best for as long as possible.

Author Dr. Roger Landry explains this message with two hypothetical characters: Andrew, who has suffered a decade and a half of pain, expensive health care costs, and dependence on others and Harold, who has an untimely end while realizing one of his lifelong dreams in Spain at eighty-six.

In short, Andrew's final period of life is an ever-growing snowball of health issues. He'd been too weak to sit up for the past year. For three years before that, he has had limited mobility after breaking his hip. Ten years before this injury, he suffered a stroke that led to difficulties in walking and speaking. Five years before Andrew's stroke, he had a mild heart attack, caused by in part by adult onset diabetes. The diabetes itself was caused by Andrew's obesity.

Harold, by contrast, is described as passionately engaged with the world and pursuing meaning and purpose until the end. Before he was struck by a drunk driver while bicycling, Harold had traveled to Spain to fulfill a lifelong dream of seeing the running of the bulls in Pamplona and had finished writing a book on American history.

Which of these lives would you choose? The answer is obvious.

Live Long, Die Short provides basic knowledge and tools to help readers cultivate a lifestyle that optimizes their health: moving more, continuing to learn and grow, maintaining and creating social connections, and having strong meaning and purpose. This lifestyle, in fact, is so basic to who we are as humans that Dr. Landry calls it living in authentic health.

Each one of us has the ability to make this large choice leading to a successful and healthy aging experience by making a lifetime of small choices (a process inspired by the Japanese concept *kaizen*). Much of *Live Long, Die Short* is devoted to helping people identify the small actions they can take now that will have a huge effect later.

Dr. Landry is a member of a team of educators, coaches, and researchers called Masterpiece Living, a revolutionary initiative that aims to make successful aging achievable for all. *Live Long, Die Short* weaves the story of Masterpiece Living's journey on this quest as a backdrop and foundation for its recommendations.

The origins of Masterpiece Living come from the MacArthur Foundation's Research Network on Successful Aging, which conducted a ten-year study beginning in 1984. Directed by Lead Investigators Drs. John Rowe and Robert Kahn, this study was the first of its kind and uncovered the remarkable truth of aging: how we age is determined more by our everyday lifestyle choices than our genes. Kahn and Rowe published their findings in *Successful Aging*. Jonas Salk, the famous developer of the polio vaccine and MacArthur Foundation Board member, praised the study findings but also identified the need to apply the results in order to realize their value to the world.

In the late 1990s, Masterpiece Living recruited Dr. Kahn and an eclectic group of academics, scientists, educators, and researchers to investigate how to best actualize the MacArthur study findings and bring them to reality.

The results of Masterpiece Living's pilot studies were stunning. Older adults participating in the study reported data in mobility, physical, intellectual, social, and spiritual parameters similar to people ten years younger. After several more years of refining their approach, which not only assisted the individual but also helped communities to develop cultures of growth and empowerment, Masterpiece Living launched its movement with partnerships across the nation.

Live Long, Die Short is written in an easy-to-understand and conversational style. The book has three sections:

The first section of *Live Long, Die Short* details the history and core philosophy behind the Masterpiece Living successful aging initiative. It provides an excellent practical approach to lifestyle change, and offers the reader tools to assess their current lifestyle.

The second section of the book contains the top ten tips that Dr. Landry and the Masterpiece Living Team have for readers. Each tip is presented with examples of people who exemplify it. These stories provide models for the reader. Mabes's story is told in "Tip Seven: Wherever You Are. . . Be There." Her story about overcoming adversity and finding peace in life illustrates the importance of mindfulness, compassion, and recognizing what we can change and what we cannot. Mabes is an excellent example of this chapter's focus on being wholly present in life.

At the end of each of these chapters, there are *Masterpiece Living Pearls*. The pearls are insightful questions and strategies to bring the suggested tip to reality in their lives. For example, one of the pearls for "Tip Four: Stay Connected" asks readers to consider what significant people may have disappeared from their lives and urges them to reconnect with those people, perhaps using social media's powerful technology. These small steps are essential to Masterpiece Living's philosophy: small choices lead to durable lifestyle changes with powerful benefits.

The third section of *Live Long, Die Short* focuses on the important implications that a growing population of older adults will have for American society, and firmly reiterates Masterpiece's commitment of bringing to reality the newly discovered possibilities for continued growth at any age.

Having taken the journey with Dr. Roger Landry, readers will feel empowered and confident. *Live Long, Die Short* has the potential to change our lives by teaching us that *we* can change our futures.

CHAPTER SUMMARIES

Foreword

The foreword is written by Dr. Robert L. Kahn, one of the founding fathers of the scientific and sociological study of successful aging. The book that he co-authored with Dr. John Rowe, *Successful Aging*, is the bedrock of the discipline.

Dr. Kahn writes about how he believes *Live Long, Die Short* is an important book because of its candor, range, and scientific validity. He praises Dr. Landry's openness and enthusiasm about empowering people so that they can achieve a better aging experience.

The foreword also expresses approval for how Dr. Landry has made his knowledge accessible to readers. He applauds the depth and practicality of the author's experience, reflecting on how Landry's career has enriched his perspective.

Lastly, Dr. Kahn commends *Masterpiece Living* for its extensive, evidence-based approach to its mission of enabling people to live their fullest, best lives. He praises the ten years of research and experiments that led to the contents of the book, and adds appreciatively that Masterpiece

Living continues to add to the growing body of knowledge in its field.

Important Quote

"Read this book. You will certainly enjoy it. You will almost certainly learn from it. And most important, it may bring you closer to attaining the ideal of its title: live long, die short." (xiii)

PART I: A NEW LOOK AT HEALTH, CHANGE, AND AGING

Chapter 1: Where Are We Now? How Did We Get Here?

Main Ideas

- Humans' social and physical requirements for health have developed over thousands of years. Since the Industrial Revolution, our society has evolved into a world where these authentic needs are elusive. In order to both be healthy and age well, we must creatively reintroduce these long-standing needs into our modern lives.

- Throughout human history, older adults served a central role in their communities; it is only recently that society has marginalized them.

Key Concepts

Authentic Health: The state of genuine vitality consistent with our human origins and individual nature. It is the result of lifestyle traits that meet our truly human needs and desires, are shared by all people, and are durable throughout our evolution. They were established over eons of our hunter-gatherer origins and persist despite the dramatic changes in how we live today.

Ageism: The discrimination and marginalization of older adults that mistakenly believes them to be "broken" versions of younger adults.

Summary

In this chapter, Dr. Landry discusses the ways that humans and their societies have evolved leading up to our current world.

Humans survived by adapting to their environment over eons within hunter-gatherer and agrarian groups and societies. These successful adaptations have been passed down to us as lifestyle requirements for health and successful aging: being physically, socially, intellectually, and spiritually engaged. Since the Industrial Revolution, our human societies and the lifestyle we live within these societies has changed radically. What we inherited from our ancestors as a lifestyle to be healthy, however, has not changed. The gap between, and how to close that gap, is the topic and target of *Live Long, Die Short*.

Dr. Landry also describes humans' social evolution. He

examines how communities treated their elders and investigates what kind of roles and responsibilities older adults had within their community. Dr. Landry looks at the different stages of human society: hunter-gather, agrarian, industrial, post-industrial.

He writes that when humans were hunter-gatherers, they connected with others, they constantly moved while searching for food, and that older members of the community had a purpose that connected with the greater good of the tribe: they guided the group, kept and passed on an oral history, and helped raise the tribe's children.

In agrarian communities, though humans settled in villages and small towns, they still moved quite a bit as they tended their pastures and livestock. Their social needs did not change, as the community was tight-knit and they depended on each other. Elders were important to their villages as advisors, historians, teachers, and child raisers.

The Industrial Revolution dramatically changed humans' social world and behaviors hundreds of thousands of years in the making. Starting only 250 years ago, or ten generations, human communities no longer found themselves working together towards a common goal—resources became deeply stratified, with laborers working long hours in dangerous conditions for the profit of the few. Rapid urbanization left many people disconnected from the earth, no longer working fields or hunting for their food. The worth of people became based on how much physical labor they could provide and their ability to produce rather than being determined by how they contributed to the bettering of a shared community. Children and older members of society were less important to production and attitudes and public policy reflected this decreased value. Older adults in particular began to be viewed as liabilities.

Though our society has changed in many ways for the better since the Industrial Revolution, our post-industrial society is markedly different from the way that humans lived during the hunter-gatherer and agrarian eras. We move little, spending most of our days sitting while we drive or at a desk while we work. We have tens, hundreds of friends but spend very little time looking them in the eyes, instead interacting via clicks and text messages. As we age, we mistakenly believe that we are leaving our "productive" years behind us, even though our life expectancy has drastically increased.

Dr. Landry ends this chapter with a look at how drastically our attitudes about aging, and our treatment of the elders in our communities, have changed. He also states that with a rapidly aging demographic, escalating health care costs for older adults, and new research on what constitutes and determines healthy aging, we must transform our current beliefs and begin to view older adulthood as a critical component of society and a growing source of human capital.

Important Quote

"[The] fact that our bodies adapt at a much slower rate than our civilization results in a maladaptation . . . this maladaptation has our bodies functioning in a 'foreign' world, has our bodies and minds desperately seeking what they need to be healthy and functioning at their best but finding it more and more difficult in a world rapidly moving away from the one our ancestors adapted to eons ago." (13)

Chapter 2: What We Know Now

Main Ideas

- How a person ages is mostly up to them. It is our lifestyle choices that increase mental and physical function and longevity while compressing time spent sick and impaired.

Key Concepts

The MacArthur Study: A study conducted on the successes of aging rather than negative aspects. This study demonstrated that how we age is mostly up to us and dispelled long-standing stereotypes that unavoidable decline is our only option.

Compression of Morbidity: The ability to increase high-functioning life expectancy while decreasing the amount of time spent sick and impaired.

Blue Zones: Locations in the world where longevity and high vitality are common.

Summary

Dr. Landry introduces the groundbreaking MacArthur Study; this study presented a revolutionary new understanding of the aging process. The study rejected the preconceived notion that aging is a decline-only experience.

Rather, the study found that successful aging decreased risk of chronic diseases, resulted in higher levels of overall function and a shorter period of terminal decline, and is primarily the result of lifestyle choices where high physical and intellectual activity are the norm, as well as lowering health risks and staying engaged with life.

Dr. Landry identifies this scenario as the Compression of Morbidity. He illustrates this idea using the stories of Andrew and Harold. Andrew spent his finals years in a long drawn-out battle against several chronic diseases while Harold adhered to lifestyle choices in line with the MacArthur Study and had a short terminal event while he was in peak health.

Chronic diseases such as Andrew's are the top causes of death in the United States. Many, if not all, of these diseases are a result of lifestyle choices and therefore are almost completely avoidable or at least modifiable. Dr. Landry assures us that it is never too late to make changes that can slow decline and enhance function.

Characteristics of successful aging include maintaining physical and cognitive functions, minimizing the risk of disease and disability, and continuing to engage with life. Dr. Landry writes that successful agers continually challenge themselves physically and intellectually in order to maintain their abilities. They take steps to identify what diseases and impairments they are at risk for, and educate themselves about the lifestyle choices that can prevent or lower the risks of being impaired. Lastly, resisting societal or self-imposed isolation with a life of meaning and purpose is a critical characteristic of aging in a better way.

These key characteristics and more can be found in Blue Zones. These locations include areas of Okinawa (Japan), Sardinia (Italy), Nicoya Peninsula (Costa Rica), and Ikaria (Greece), as well as Loma Linda, California. They are characterized by high vitality and longevity and reflect lifestyles similar to ancestral societies and those identified by the MacArthur Study.

The similarities in these cultures validate the importance of the MacArthur Study and its conclusion that individuals can influence the quality and quantity of their lives.

Dr. Landry ends this chapter with the idea that we are the maestros of our own lives. He says that we are much like the conductor of a symphony; it is our job to coordinate our physical, mental, social, and spiritual needs, making necessary adjustments to maintain harmony.

Important Quote

"It is the choices we make every day that will determine whether we live the last decades of our lives slowly deteriorating, impaired and isolated, or continuing to grow, accommodating life's curveballs, staying vital and flourishing." (40)

Chapter 3: Can We Change?

Main Ideas

- Lifestyle change is very difficult because we often attempt too radical a change. Evolving small changes are more successful and durable.

Key Concepts

Transtheoretical Model of Behavior Change: A six-step model used by professionals to guide clients through behavioral change.

Fight or Flight Response: An inherited behavior used as a survival skill by our ancestors as a reaction to immediate danger that demands an immediate response.

Kaizen: A Japanese technique for making change, in personal lives or business, that involves making small evolving changes in order to achieve lasting goals.

Summary

Chapter three focuses on the concept of change. Despite the fact that we know change is an unavoidable part of life, we tend to resist it and spend much time and energy erecting barriers to change.

Part of the reason we balk at the idea of change is because it inherently involves moving to the unknown. And the unknown is scary. Despite our amazing ability to adapt, we have a constant fear that we will fail or not survive change. We find comfort in ritual, which brings us a sense of peace with our surroundings.

We inherited this from our ancestors, who valued ritual and saw large change as a threat. This was accompanied by fear and stress. Successful agers make constant small life-style changes throughout their lives that help prevent that instinctive "fight or flight" response and make change more attainable and durable.

Professor James O. Prochaska at the University of Rhode Island developed a *Transtheoretical Model of Behavior Change* that professionals use to assesses readiness for change. The model identifies six stages: The *precontemplative* stage, the *contemplative* stage, the *preparation* stage, the *action* stage, the *maintenance* stage, and the *termination* stage.

There are two major obstacles to successfully changing. The first is our inherent resistance to major change. Our fear of change runs deep and is connected to our inherited flight-or-fight response. For hunter-gatherer societies, fear was a necessary survival skill that kick-started the necessary mental and physical responses to meet the challenge producing fear.

The part of the brain responsible this survival response is the "middle brain" or the "paleomammalian brain." This section of our brain, the amygdala in particular, releases neurotransmitters telling the body to either fight or take flight from a situation. It shuts down other body systems in order for us to concentrate on the immediate threat. However, when we generate fear by taking on large change, even when it's not life threatening, we shut down capabilities necessary to achieve the change.

The second obstacle to successful change is our tendency to value only major changes. Often we set goals for ourselves that are too ambitious. Setting these high goals, again, triggers our fear response and with it some higher function necessary to achieve change successfully.

Kaizen is the answer to obtaining the change we want and need to make. The Japanese technique advocates small changes and goals that are easy to achieve. The amygdala will not go into fight-or-flight mode and therefore not generate fear or stress in the face of these changes, giving us a higher chance of achieving success. *Kaizen* is about asking small questions, taking small steps, and solving small problems. These small successes build on each other and ultimately allow us to achieve larger goals and change.

Important Quote

"Kaizen is about taking small steps. Having asked ourselves small questions, decided what small action we might do to change our lives, and used mind sculpture to practice that action and begin to make brain connections that will make it easy to perform, we now take small steps toward our goal." (53)

Chapter 4: Your Personal Lifestyle Inventory

Main Idea

- Once you evaluate your current lifestyle, you can begin to address the areas of your authentic lifestyle that are missing.

Key Concepts

Personal Lifestyle Inventory: a series of questions that guide readers through their lifestyle self-assessment.

Summary

Dr. Landry takes the readers through the process of assessing whether their current lifestyles are likely to lead to healthy aging. He provides them with a detailed Personal Lifestyle Inventory that asks them easy-to-answer questions about the various parts of their lives that are connected to successful aging. These questions are simple to answer yet very revealing, opening up an excellent opportunity to make substantive and valuable lifestyle change.

Questions include:

1. How much total time do you spend moving your body during an average day (walking, exercising, doing physical work)?

2. How many people did you share a face-to-face conversation with today that lasted longer than two minutes?

3. How many days last week did you learn something new or do something you've never done before?

4. Are you proud of your answer when someone asks how you spend your day?

5. How many servings of fruits, vegetables, or nuts do you eat most days?

6. What is the difference between your current weight and what you weighed at age eighteen?

7. How many times today did you feel in a rush?

8. How much do you worry?

9. How often are you thinking about things other than what you're currently doing?

10. Are you pleased with the quality of your sleep?

11. How many times did you laugh today (not just smile, but laugh for longer than two seconds)?

12. How long has it been since you last interacted with a child?

Readers answer questions, can score their lifestyle inventory, and receive feedback and guidance regarding next steps.

Landry then gives them advice on how to get the most out of the second section of *Live Long, Die Short*.

For example, if someone chooses the answer "(B) Weeks" to the previous question about interacting with a child, then Dr. Landry advises them to consult Tips Nine and Ten. Each of the questions in the inventory has this level of detail in its scoring, making the chapter extremely insightful.

Additionally, each answer is weighted. For some questions, answer A may be worth five points and answer B may be worth eight points. At the end of the inventory, readers create their cumulative lifestyle inventory score. This score represents their authentic health score. The process is non-threatening. Dr. Landry provides conversational, easy-to-follow, recommendations and further instructions in this second section of *Live Long, Die Short*.

Important Quote

"The hard part is answering [these questions] truthfully. Your answers will help guide you to the best recommendations for aging in a better way, a more enjoyable way, a more successful way. There are no right answers, only *your* answers." (56)

PART II: TEN TIPS TO ACHIEVE AUTHENTIC HEALTH AND SUCCESSFUL AGING

Tip 1: Use It or Lose It

Main Ideas

- We must consistently use the physical, emotional, and social skills we wish to keep as we age.

Summary

If we wish to be all that we can be for as long as possible, then we must intentionally and continually reinforce those lifestyle elements shown to more likely result in a successful aging experience.

Intentionality is important because, as Dr. Landry says, "We don't usually choose to not use something." When we find ourselves struggling to remember details or struggling with actions that used to be second nature, it is most often the result having neglected an aspect of our lives. One of the best ways to be able to recover quickly from injuries or setbacks, in fact, is to be strong in all areas of our lives. These ten tips help us to do just that.

Technology, although expanding our lives in many ways, can make it easy for us to neglect important physical, emotional, and social skills, resulting in "losing" those skills.

Selected Masterpiece Living Pearls

- Picture yourself on a typical day in five years: What does the day involve? How much walking? What brain and physical skills? What other people are involved?

Make a personal lifestyle plan for each of these skills or abilities. Remember, this is going to take some time; think *small steps*. What little actions can you add to each day to sharpen these skills for the future?

Important Quote

"What we don't use tends to go the way of a discarded bicycle, left out in the elements. It basically rusts to the point where it is no longer usable. We lose the ability to do what we could before." (79)

Tip 2: Keep Moving

Main Ideas

- Physical activity, which has been systematically removed from our daily lives, is a fundamental requirement for successful aging.

Summary

Movement is critical to health and successful aging. Most of us, however, live a sedentary lifestyle, which is the silent enemy, linked to prevalent chronic diseases. Once a disease impairs us, we tend to decrease movement that then leads to more chronic disease. It is a vicious cycle that can be prevented.

Movement was a fundamental characteristic of our ancestors' lives. Our high-tech lifestyles have provided us much opportunity to avoid regular daily movement. Even when we "work out" it is usually a scheduled event lasting only a small part of our otherwise sedentary day.

Movement is an easily modifiable lifestyle choice. Simply walking could help prevent cancer and increase life expectancy. Using the concept of kaizen, we can start by walking just five minutes a day and gradually increasing movement until it becomes an innate part of our day. Doing this will help us lower our risk of heart disease, cancer, Alzheimer's, arthritis, and other impairments.

Selected Masterpiece Living Pearls

- Take note of how many steps you take each day using a step counter. Find the daily average number of steps over a three-day period. Then, set a goal for increasing that daily amount using the principles of Kaizen, i.e., increasing steps by ever progressing small amounts.

- Take note of how you spend your time being sedentary or moving. Evaluate your routine and reorganize your time to include purposeful movement. It does not have to be sweat-inducing exertion; you just need to move.

Important Quote

"Movement is, for us as a species, closer to our real selves, our authentic selves." (93)

Tip 3: Challenge Your Brain

Main Ideas

- With the discovery of *neuroplasticity,* the brain's lifelong ability to rewire itself, we've come to understand that the brain is not a stagnant organ that inevitably declines in function over time. Rather, the brain has the capacity to adjust and grow in function throughout life as long as we continually challenge it.

Summary

Our brains are not stagnant organs destined for inevitable decline. Neuroplasticity provides our brains the ability to change and grow when we stimulate it through learning and experience. We are the architects of our own brains.

Neuroplasticity allows our brain to rewire itself in response to injury, disease, or challenge. Each time we learn something new—a new song, a language, how to play an instrument—we create new neural pathways. If we continue to challenge our brain, we will maintain and grow new pathways which allow us to function well into old age.

In the event of injury, such as stroke, we may lose those pathways created and not be able to function as we did before. However, due to neuroplasticity, new pathways can be created and allow our brains to relearn some of the functions.

Not only can our brain rebuild connections, it can also make new cells through neurogenesis. Studies have shown that new cells only survive when we incorporate them into new pathways by learning new things.

Selected Masterpiece Living Pearls

- Learn something new. Whether it is learning a few words of a new language, a new song, or finding a new route to the grocery store, do something different. Habits stagnate the brain, even if they seem comforting and familiar. It's not about becoming an expert in something. It doesn't matter if you fail. Start something new. Be a beginner.

- Our diets affect our brain function. Obesity is associated with higher risk for dementia. Our brains function better with a diet composed of whole grains, fish, fruits, nuts and vegetables.

- De-stress your brain. Seek out activities that quiet the incessant chatter in the brain and instead provide peace and enjoyment. Your chosen activities should focus the mind and help pass the time joyfully rather than rotting the brain with stress.

Important Quote

"The road to excellent brain health is pretty much the road to overall health, and that road is a lifestyle that pays attention to our physical, spiritual, and social health as well as the intellectual." (106)

Tip 4: Stay Connected

Main Ideas

- We humans have a basic need to be connected with others in order to thrive.

Summary

Connection with others is a fundamental need for us to thrive. It was a survival necessity for our ancestors and it remains in us as a health and successful aging one.

Social interaction is a core value of our authentic selves and is critical to aging well. Keeping older adults on the fringes of society, or otherwise isolated, is a post-Industrial Revolution anomaly both foreign and destructive to who we are as humans.

High-tech brain scanning further proves that we are wired to be social creatures. When we observe emotion in others, our own neurons in similar regions of the brain respond. These mirror neurons reflect empathy and the neurologic basis for our connection to others.

Connectedness not only makes us feel better, it makes us healthier. Studies show that we are more likely to die prematurely from all major causes if we are socially disconnected compared with others who have close ties to others. Depression, dementia, and overall stress are less frequent with regular social contact.

Blue Zones, areas of the world where we observe both longevity and vitality, represent societies that value older adults and encourage engagement and integration throughout the life span.

It is important to note that although the digital era has increased our ability to "connect" to others, talking on the phone, texting, and keeping in touch through other technological means do not fully meet our core need for social engagement. Face-to-face interaction and touch provide the most powerful health benefits for us.

Selected Masterpiece Living Pearls

- Evaluate the people in your life that stimulate and energize you. Surround yourself with meaningful connections that nurture you.

- Identify the people in your life who drain you. Purge your life of, or limit the time you spend with, those who make you feel bad about yourself or others or the world.

- Take inventory of the number of people in your life. Doing the things you love to do and being open to others can increase that number.

Important Quote

"People who are socially disconnected or isolated are between two and five times more likely to die from *all causes* compared to matched individuals who have close ties with family, friends and community." (114)

Tip 5: Lower your Risks

Main Ideas

- We cannot ignore our lifestyle risks. We must first identify what they are and then manage them with knowledge and the assistance of experts.

Summary

Part of being responsible for our lifestyle, and hence our
health and aging, is to know our risks and manage them.
Most diseases affecting us today are caused primarily by
lifestyle and can be prevented by adopting healthy habits
and taking preventive measures to eliminate or reduce them
in order to build resilience.

When we are younger, we are healthy because of our
youth with its emphasis on vanity, performance, or attract-
ing a mate. As we age we often slowly slip into unhealthy
habits, accepting decline as inevitable. But decline is not
inevitable. Dr. Landry discusses two areas associated with
high risk and which are modifiable.

The first, stress, is linked to our fight-or-flight response.
Our ancestors faced threats that required immediate response
in order to survive. Today, we don't face the same threats as

our ancestors, but our frenetic lifestyles and chattering minds replicate those same threats, creating toxic stress-filled environments that result in higher risks for all major diseases.

We can, however, mitigate stress and minimize its effects with mindfulness, physical activity, social connection, adequate sleep, and eating well.

How we eat is another major area of potential risk. We eat to live and function well. The diet of our ancestors—fruits, nuts, vegetables, beans, wild grains, fish, and small amounts of meat—was the core diet of our species for eons and remains today as the core of our nutritional needs. It is nutrition, rather than weight, that should drive our choice. Obesity is a huge risk factor for not only heart disease and diabetes, but also cancer and dementia. Ideal weight will follow proper nutrition and regular movement.

Aristotle told us "all things in moderation" and this rings true even today. By following a Mediterranean-type diet on which we as humans have survived and thrived, moving regularly, and consuming high caloric foods only in moderation, we can significantly reduce our risk for chronic disease and rapid decline.

Knowledge is power for living authentically, in addition to managing stress and maintaining a nutritious diet. The lifestyle embedded in the ten tips in this book can keep us healthy and aging well. And, as we are now learning, it can even override genetic risks by potentially putting disease-causing genes to sleep.

Of course, regular checkups, cancer screenings, and working with your doctor to lower risks are sensible components of a successful aging strategy.

Selected Masterpiece Living Pearls

- Use the Lifestyle Inventory to assess your personal risks. Once you've identified your risks, consult your physician to pinpoint your risk level and work with them to take action to reverse, manage, or prevent disease.

- Take notes and evaluate your eating habits over a few days. Consider what you would like to change and set small goals in order to reach your desired outcome.

Important Quotes

"And indeed the list of illnesses and conditions related to chronic stress is impressive because the adverse effects of chronic stress involve the cardiovascular system, the brain, and the immune system itself." (129)

"Our core needs are about nourishment. Our approach to authentic health is not about deprivation, but about providing for our core nutritional needs." (131)

Tip 6: Never "Act Your Age"

Main Ideas

- We should not let anyone dictate how we should age or
  what expectations we have for aging. As long as we keep
  growing physically, mentally, socially, and spiritually, we
  will be successfully aging.

Summary

Growing older in our society is often viewed as being all
about decline only. We do not have to "act our age," because
doing that is buying into this stereotype. Only we should set
expectations for our aging. As long as we continually grow,
we will be successful.

Society devalues the potential in older adults, seeing
them as impaired and broken beings. In other societies, like
Okinawa, older adults are revered and an essential part of
the community. This comes, however, with a responsibility,
called *yurimaru*, or reciprocity. Older adults are valued, but
also expected to continue to contribute as teachers, men-
tors, and guides.

Environment is a critical factor in influencing our aging
process. Adults who were surrounded by negative opinions
about aging and focused only on comfort and security are

less successful in aging. Conversely, older adults who reside in communities that counter ageism show physical, intellectual, social, and spiritual growth.

We must challenge ourselves and take risks and even do things that scare us. When we take ourselves out of our comfort zone, we grow. Our immune system, brain, and muscles respond and grow with change.

We can even turn back the clock by acting like our much younger selves. If we stay active and continue to do things we expected to do for ourselves when we were young, our brain and body will respond to actualize that expectation. Our brain will rewire itself and signal the body that it is much younger and more adept than our actual age. If we expect decline and less functionality, that will most likely be our reality. Higher expectations yield higher function.

Selected Masterpiece Living Pearls

- Do something you've always wanted to do. It should be something of significance that you've given much thought to, but never did. Do something you've given up ever doing because you became "too old." Travel somewhere exotic. Learn a new language or how to play an instrument. Challenge yourself.

- Do something that scares you. Challenge yourself to something that you've always avoided and use small steps to overcome it. Avoiding things due to fear limits your potential. Once you identify your fear, you can take steps to overcome it and then continue to grow.

Important Quotes

"Even when given with the best intentions, the advice to 'act our age' throws water on the embers of our potential." (142)

"Creating places that respect and value older adults, that help them believe in their potential, and that incorporate them into the very fabric of the community is what Masterpiece Living has been doing, and is dedicated to continue." (142-143)

Tip 7: Wherever You Are...Be There

Main Ideas

- Most of our stress is self-induced, the product of our unwillingness to acknowledge reality and the inevitability of change. This stress rots us from within, making us more likely to be unhealthy and age poorly.

- We are our own obstacles to attaining spiritual growth. We allow the stress and incessant chatter in our brains to keep us from being present in our own spiritual journey.

Summary

Our spiritual health is just as important to aging successfully as the physical, social, and intellectual components. Spirituality is our quest for understanding the meaning of our life and our relationship with the universe. The answers themselves, however, are not as important as the journey to find them. As we age, we become less concerned about materialistic or rational things and more about more transcendent matters. This period is called *gerotranscendence* and is often accompanied by an increase in life satisfaction.

So what is stopping us from embarking on this joyous

journey? Our human mind can be that impediment. Our mind tends to race with thoughts that keep us from being present in the moment. When our thoughts are consumed with the past or future, guilt, anxiety, regret, and sadness take hold and we are unable to experience the peace and joy of being present in the moment.

In order to travel a spiritual journey, we must first learn to quiet our chattering thoughts and settle in a place referred to by Buddhists as "no mind." This place can last only moments but is a powerful tool to manage our stress. Such moments can be found in nature, creative arts, meditation, and other mindful pursuits. Breaking the incessant, stress-producing treadmill of destructive thought, even for seconds, can make all the difference in the quality of our lives.

Selected Masterpiece Living Pearls

- Try meditation. This is a simple act can quiet the mind chatter that keeps us from being in the moment. Start with just a few minutes and don't give up if thoughts interrupt your attempts. Keep at it and you can extend the "no mind" time. Pair this with yoga, tai chi, or qigong to assist in calming runaway thoughts. These physical practices will also help improve balance, strength, and flexibility while bringing you inner peace.

- Be mindful of the fact that there are only three ways to deal with a problem you encounter: fix it, leave it, or accept it. All else is madness . . . and destructive to our bodies, minds, and souls.

Important Quote

"Our unique ability, or perhaps curse, to generate a stress response with our thoughts and reactions to a rushing, time-dominated world to which we have not yet biologically adapted is indeed one of the main themes of this book." (155)

Tip 8: Find Your Purpose

Main Ideas

- It is important for us to continue finding purpose throughout our lifetime. Without it, we wither and lose resilience.

Summary

As we age, we must resist stagnation and instead seek our *generativity*: "a concern for establishing and guiding the next generation." Basically, we must find a reason to get out of bed in the morning. Most meaning and purpose involves other living things, but only we can define what is meaningful to us. We may find value in volunteering to help others in need, growing a garden, tutoring children, or learning a craft. The point is that it needs to fulfill our own needs. Our values can change over time. What we once thought of as a purposeful pursuit in our youth may be redefined with newly acquired wisdom and experiences.

Volunteerism can be a meaningful activity. Not only can it bring us purpose, but research has found it brings us longer, higher-quality life. Helping others makes us happy, even joyful, and significantly increases our resilience.

Selected Masterpiece Living Pearls

- Identify activities you engaged in earlier in life before responsibilities took precedence. Find opportunities to rediscover these areas of interest in order to gain a sense of fulfillment.

- Do not hold yourself back by thinking that your purpose must be a prodigious undertaking. The only attribute of your chosen purpose is that it is meaningful for you and brings you joy. Even if it is new and scary, you'll be better for it.

Important Quote

"Whether it's growing roses or lobbying to eliminate land mines, feeding birds or being politically active, picking up litter or saving the whales, you are the judge, the ultimate authority on what has meaning for you and therefore what will bring you satisfaction and even joy, and with that, a better aging experience." (164)

Tip 9: Have Children in Your Life

Main Ideas

- Intergenerational contact has been the rule of our species and remains necessary for both young and old to be whole and more healthy.

Summary

Tip Nine addresses the significance of older adult interaction with children and young adults. Intergenerational relationships are the core of a healthy society, allowing for the transfer of knowledge, experience, and wisdom of the old to young; meaning and purpose in the third stage of life; and infusion of the joy, optimism, and passion of the young into the lives of older adults at high risk for isolation and despair.

Our connection to children, however, is also linked to our personal health. As we age, we can potentially become more marginalized and isolated, and our risk for chronic disease and impairment rises. As noted earlier, this is related to lack of social connection as well as meaning and purpose. Since the beginning of our history as humans, older adults played a major role in the maturation of children. Removal from connection to the young, then, is an interruption in the very circle of life, depriving older adults not only of the role as mentor but also the spiritual role as an elder. Dostoyevsky told us "the soul is healed by being with children."

When children thrive, so does the rest of society. As we mentor them and benefit from the interaction, so will the rest of society. Children are less likely to make negative lifestyle choices like taking drugs or engaging in violent behaviors when they are part of programs like the Big Brothers Big Sisters of America.

Selected Masterpiece Living Pearls

- Start small by spending time with the children in your family. Simply interact with them without any planned activities or agenda. Give them the gift of your time.

- Volunteer your time at child-centric places. Visit schools and libraries to tutor children. Visit hospitals to keep young patients company or help with newborns. Sign up for programs such as Big Brothers and Big Sisters and become a mentor for a child in need.

Important Quote

"When we look beyond the complex parent-child relationship, with its focus on safety, discipline, and providing for needs, we can allow the relationship to be what it is, if only for short periods of time: two humans, in different places on a circle, yet connected, and both necessary to maintain the circle of life." (174)

Tip 10: Laugh to a Better Life

Main Ideas

- Laughter is associated with a better aging experience. The reasons are just now becoming clear but increased social interactions, positive physical effects, and a more robust immunologic system probably play a role. Optimistic people tend to live seven and a half years longer than negative people.

Summary

One of the simplest steps to age in a better way is to laugh.

Laughter is a core human signaling system. It is part of a basic human vocabulary, and even babies and other primates can recognize its meaning. Not only is it easily recognizable, it is also an inherently positive social connector that is strongly associated with better health and longevity. Cases of major health improvement related to laughter are outlined in *Live Long, Die Short*.

Laughter releases beta-endorphins, which can positively affect our mood, are a major stress reducer, reduce pain, allow us to share a common experience with others, and are an immunological booster. This, in turn, reduces our risk of infectious disease, cancer, heart disease, depression, and even dementia.

Selected Masterpiece Living Pearls

- Identify how you present yourself to the world. Notice the difference between when you are conscious of how you portray yourself versus your default look. Make an effort to not lapse into a neutral face that is often interpreted as sad or angry. Smile and present a more positive neutral look to the world. It will improve your interactions with others.

- Spend more time with those with whom you laugh more and less time with those who are consistently negative.

Important Quote

"Laughter seems to boost our immune system, which has the potential to assist us in resisting cancer and infection, as well as a number of other threats to our good health and successful aging, and we feel much better while all this is happening." (179)

PART III: WHERE DO WE GO FROM HERE?

Chapter 16: A Look Into Our Future: It Won't Be What You Think

Main Ideas

- We will begin to see the inevitable shift from the marginalization of older adults to inclusion as our population of older adults (those reaching age sixty-five) continues to grow at a rate of eight thousand per day over the next twelve years. Older adults will become elders with a sense of responsibility to contribute and give back to society as a whole. Our society, on the other hand, will view its elders as human capital and, as in the Blue Zones, as cultural treasures.

Key Concepts

Intergenerational Strife: A potential conflict arising between generations as the older adult population grows with a heavier burden on the young to support it.

Eldertopia: A concept of community described by Dr. Bill Thomas in which the quality of life for all ages is improved by strengthening and improving the means by which the community protects, sustains, and nurtures its elders, who then contribute to the well-being and foresight of the community, advancing the good of all.

Tipping Point: A concept in the book *The Tipping Point* by Malcolm Gladwell that states major change happens when a particular threshold is reached. Dr. Landry posits that we are nearing the tipping point of a societal or cultural shift in which elders will reenter society as a source of human capital for guidance, mentoring, volunteerism, and overall perspective.

Age Wave: A book by Dr. Ken Dychtwald that foretells the changes that will inevitably occur within our society as a wave of baby boomers turn sixty-five at a rate of over eight thousand per day over the next twelve years.

Summary

In chapter sixteen Dr. Landry describes how demographics, combined with the new knowledge that we can age in a better way, will change our world. With a rate of more than eight thousand people turning sixty-five every day over the next twelve years, it is inevitable that this huge source of human capital cannot and will not be ignored.

Under our current practice of marginalizing older adults, with longer life expectancy these older adults will have longer periods of entitlement support. Some intergenerational strife is possible as the ratio of retired to workers grows. There clearly must be a shift in responsibility. As they rise in influence, elders will take responsibility for the group and, rather than promoting a self-serving approach to policy change, will shepherd us towards the common good. A community that strengthens and improves quality of life by nurturing its elders and encouraging their contributions is referred to as an *Eldertopia* in Dr. Bill Thomas's recent book by the same title.

Our new world will empower older adults as they realize the possibilities of aging successfully and lead them to demand opportunity to grow, find purpose, and engage in society in order to make a difference. The rhetoric used when referencing older adults will also change with this shift. Stereotypical phrasing associated with decline will disappear as both older adults and society begin to engage the experience capital, poised to improve the lives of all.

Older adults will seek out lifestyles that promote successful aging: more social connection, physical activity, and continued learning. They will also aggressively seek out opportunities to find meaning and purpose, engaging in political and social activism, volunteerism, and mentoring. It will be experience that will be valued more than comfort and security alone. As we age, we will seek opportunities that enhance our spiritual, mental, social, and physical authentic needs.

The shift toward an Eldertopia is moving steadily toward a tipping point. The context that favors change is present in our society and powerful. When we reach this tipping point, the aging of America will be viewed as a solution rather than a problem.

Important Quote

"Time spent helping other living things in their journey through life will offer satisfaction, as always, but our enlightened older adults will also realize that the quality, and perhaps even quantity, of their own lives will be enriched." (198)

Chapter 17: A Moral Imperative: When There's Really No Choice

Main Ideas

- Now that we know that we can enjoy a higher quality of life while avoiding a painful decline if we make appropriate lifestyle choices, we face a choice to age in the usual way or remain the best we can be for longer and longer. Moreover, as a society we face a moral and social imperative to enact policies that will facilitate more positive aging for all.

Key Concepts

Four-minute mile: A metaphor used to describe the barrier in possibilities for aging. It was thought that no one could ever run a mile in less than four minutes . . . until Roger Bannister did. And today we have high schoolers doing it.

Moral High Ground: The position that caregiving communities take when defending a traditional medical model for older adults. The new demographic and research-driven possibilities now challenge that view. The moral imperative to assist all in being all they can be by continuing growing is the new moral high ground.

Summary

In this chapter, Dr. Landry lays down the gauntlet of successful aging to all who work with older adults. The research is clear: much more is possible; lifestyle is the major determinant and can even affect genetic influence. At the current rate of demographic change and health care costs, our society will be crushed by the burden of aging. But we need not be. Dr. Landry insists that a paradigm shift in the way we view older adults is a moral imperative. He uses the idea of the four-minute mile as a metaphor for the barriers we face when considering this change. Before 1954, nobody had ever run a mile in less than four minutes. Since that record was broken, under-four-minute miles are routine. We know we can live longer and die shorter. As individuals and as a society, we must move towards realizing this possibility for all.

Much of this resistance to transitioning into growth-centric models is fear based. Understanding the possibilities for life long growth will change this. Older adults will be drawn to live in communities that value them and realize that growth is possible throughout the entire lifespan.

We humans most often feel obligated to make the world a better place and improve the human condition. As Dr. Landry states, the definition of moral imperative is "the obligation to make something happen because we know it is the right thing." Society is defined by how we treat our elders and children. We would not choose to limit our children's growth. How can we then not promote the same for older adults? Are we not all aging?

Important Quote

"Not only is it advantageous for a society to have high-functioning, fulfilled, and engaged citizens, but with healthcare costs exponentially increasing and threatening the financial stability and strategic growth of the nation, doesn't it seem plausible that public policy should reflect a commitment to assist people in preventing disease and decline, and in continuing to be viable and engaged?" (208-209)

Chapter 18: Bringing "What If?" to Reality: The Rest of the Masterpiece Living Story

Main Ideas

- Masterpiece Living is leading a social movement to improve the aging experience for all. Using its experience and data, this group is committed to influencing not only individual lives, but the public policy that can enhance our society.

Key Concepts

Movement: Masterpiece Living is considered a movement rather than a program, as it encapsulates a fundamental paradigm shift in how we approach aging.

Culture: The most important component of the Masterpiece Living movement. This concept posits that successful aging takes place in an environment free of ageism, one that fosters the continued growth of older adults no matter what challenges they meet in their aging journey.

Summary

In this chapter, Dr. Landry continues the story of Masterpiece Living's journey to enrich the lives of all older adults.

When the team began in 1999, they were facing the dominant stereotype that aging meant decline. The aging service industry and public policy chose to concentrate on caring, comfort, and security. The idea of growth and potential in aging adults was rarely considered.

They began the daunting task of overcoming this mindset with a research-based, data-driven approach. The first step was to develop tools to help older adults take a look at their current lifestyle and determine where they were at risk. With this information and a coaching option within a community that supported continued growth—much like a university offers its students—older adults then began to make small changes in lifestyle which led to lasting change, which in turn led to a more functional and fulfilling third stage of life.

The approach is simple: Educate older adults about the possibilities new research provided, offer them the Lifestyle Inventory and the feedback, discuss the feedback, coach them on empowerment of their potential, turn them loose within an environment that supported their growth and successful aging, and follow the journey with data on their outcomes.

The results were even better than they hoped, with significant reduction in risk and an overall improvement in health. Moving forward, Dr. Landry and his team came to the realization that Masterpiece Living had to be more than just another wellness program. A paradigm shift towards a culture that promotes continued growth throughout life, even with impairments—a culture without ageism—was also the goal. This was indeed a movement.

Masterpiece Living has continued to grow in size and influence. Now in more than eighty senior living communities, Masterpiece Living is beginning to partner with any organization feeling the challenge of an aging society: churches, residential country clubs, cities and towns. Partnering with similarly motivated professional groups, Masterpiece Living is making a difference, and has data to document that difference. Knowing that the vast majority of older adults will remain in the homes where they have lived for decades, Masterpiece Living will soon be reaching out via the web to these people also. Offering tried and true resources, now refined for use in this digital world, this new approach will allow them to realize the original vision: "A society in which aging means growth, engagement, vitality, and purpose."

Important Quote

"Aging as growing is an idea whose time has come, and the seismic nature of what it can mean for individuals and societies is palpable." (220)

Conclusion:
The Time of Our Lives…Really

Summary

This concluding chapter begins with a Jack London quote about living life to the fullest . . . to live fully rather than to just exist.

Dr. Landry challenges readers to do the same: to take responsibility for our lives. By following his ten tips and using the principles of kaizen, we are certain not to fail in our path to a better aging journey. We will improve our health, reduce our stress, improve our physical functionality, and enhance brain function, making us less vulnerable to disease of the body, mind, and spirit.

Dr. Landry cautions us that if indeed life throws us a curveball and we are somewhat impaired, that does not mean we have failed in our journey to successful aging. It is our response that is important. We must deal with it, but accommodate the new reality, asking ourselves: What can I do to keep at maximum level of functioning? What can I do to prevent or limit further decline?

This book is a call to action. Each of us is responsible for achieving successful aging. We must acknowledge our part in aging and shift our view on what it means to be an older adult in society. We must, as individuals and as a society, recognize the abilities and potential of older adults to contribute positively. When we succeed, our success will ripple through the community and become a wave of positive movement toward better lives for all, where all have the possibility to live long and die short.

Important Quote

"When you succeed in your life, when others succeed, when organizations succeed, when towns and cities succeed, it becomes a movement, paving the way for changes in public policy that will make aging a journey of wonder, adventure, and continued growth, policy that will make aging as colorful as New England fall leaves, where everyone has the possibility of living long and dying short." (225)

ABOUT THE AUTHOR

Dr. Roger Landry is a preventive medicine physician who specializes in building environments that empower older adults to maximize their unique potential. Trained at Tufts University School of Medicine and Harvard University School of Public Health, he is the president of Masterpiece Living, a group of multidiscipline specialists in aging who partner with communities to help them become destinations for continued growth.

Dr. Landry was a flight surgeon in the Air Force for over twenty-two years, and one of his charges was world famous test pilot, Chuck Yeager. Dr. Landry retired as a highly decorated full colonel and chief flight surgeon at the Air Force Surgeon General's Office in Washington, DC, after duty on five continents and being medically involved in a number of significant world events including Vietnam, the Chernobyl nuclear disaster, the Beirut bombing of the Marine barracks, the first seven shuttle launches, and the first manned balloon crossing of the Pacific.

For the last decade, Dr. Landry has focused his efforts on older adults as a lecturer, researcher, consultant, and author. He lives on Cape Cod.

A ROUSING CALL TO RETHINK THE AGING PROCESS

Made in the USA
Monee, IL
08 October 2020

44350525R00037